21 ½ Things to Know Before Self-publishing a Book

By Mike Swedenberg

Copyright © 2016 James Michael Swedenberg

ISBN-13: 978-1535199735

ISBN-10: 1535199733

DEDICATION
To all those with a story to tell

Contents

"Being a writer is like having homework every night
for the rest of your life."
Lawrence Kasdan

Forward

The following is my lesson plan presented to Writers at

Nassau Community College and other

Continuing Education Institutions.

A Training Nightmare

I worked for a publishing company that would only hire experienced sales reps from other publishing companies with specific track record in the Legal Market (Selling Law and Tax Books)

They sent us to Sales Training 101 run by an instructor with zero sales experience who used an off-the-shelf generic training lesson.

She was the least experienced person in the room and had only recently joined the company. She had no product knowledge and could not answer any of our questions. Nevertheless, the company pulled us out of the sales field, sent to the home office for a week of Sales 101. We had to sit there and listen to her drone on about things she knew nothing about.

At the end of the class, an evaluation test revealed the number one sales representative in the country had poor selling skills while the lowest ranked reps excelled.

This experience has motivated me to outline my background and qualifications. To earn the right to offer you my advice.

My Background
Education

Adelphi University BS Business and Management

School of Visual Arts Advertising Copywriting and Design

Gotham School of Writing

Career

Ten years Advertising Copywriting and Production

Sixteen years sales, marketing in Publishing for global companies

Four years as a Continuing Ed Instructor

My Courses at Nassau Community College, Garden City NY

NEW HOW TO PUBLISH AN E-BOOK

Become a published author in as little as four weeks. Your novel, how-to book, short story, cookbook or memoir will be published by eleven online book sellers including Amazon.com and Barnes and Noble for free. The step-by-step process will be explained in simple everyday language. Topics include format, book cover design, short and long descriptions, key words, pricing and marketing. This is a high energy laboratory course requiring full participation by all. Students should have a project ready or near ready to publish in which they own full copyright. A complete syllabus will be furnished by email. Get published now rather than never.

Required materials: access to MS Word 1997 or later, Windows XP or later, and a thumb drive.

NEW 15 THINGS YOU NEED TO KNOW BEFORE SELF-PUBLISHING A BOOK

So many have a book inside them but few know how to go about writing and self-publishing it the right way. Many writers set out with the best intentions to write their book only to learn that they have spent a year creating a file in the wrong format. This seminar will guide the writers on avoiding costly mistakes in formatting, choosing a publisher, royalties and marketing.

HOW TO PUBLISH YOUR BOOK IN PRINT ON CREATESPACE (CED 9551 B1)

NEW

Amazon's CreateSpace offers a print-on-demand service with no set-up fees to online retailers, bookstores, libraries, academic institutions, and distributors worldwide. There is no cost for publishing on CreateSpace, however, the process is daunting to a first time writer. This course simplifies the process. Learn the fundamentals of self-publishing a Print on Demand (POD) and eBook simultaneously through one of the world's largest POD publishers. Topics include production, cover design, creating a description, and keywords. The course is a combination of lectures and hands-on lab work.

Published Works

Study Guides to the US Immigration Test in 12 Languages

Bi Lingual editions available in Print and eBooks:

Spanish, Polish, French, Portuguese, Russian, Bosnian, Korean, Vietnamese, Chinese, Albanian, Arabic and Tagalog.

Novels

A New York Wedding

Bully Boss

The Short Stories of Mike Swedenberg

Non Fiction

The Sales Rep Survival Guide

The Road Warrior

Advertising Copywriting and the Unique Selling Proposition

21 1/2 Things to Know Before Self-publishing a Book: 2016

My Total – thus far

28 titles in print, eBooks and one CD with worldwide distribution.

What Do Independent Authors earn?

Individual author earnings tracked across seven quarters,

Feb. 2014 – Sept. 2015

Source: http://authorearnings.com/report/individual-author-earnings-tracked-across-7-quarters-feb-2014-sept-2015/

> Title-level data spanning half a billion eBook purchases, nearly $3 billion in consumer eBook spending, and a billion dollars in author earnings.

> 5,643 authors in our longitudinal data set — or roughly 2.8% of the original 200,000 — whose Kindle best-selling eBooks appearing on Amazon best seller lists were consistently earning them $10K/year or better.

In summary

I sell about 400 books a month on Amazon generating a five figure annual income. I started with eBooks in 2010 and then added print in 2015. I tripled my print sales overnight by changing my TAGS

**If I can do it you can too, but it takes effort
and constant study.**

Mandatory Reading

Why these books?

You need to learn what the professionals look for in submitted work and how they weed out the bad writers.

By understanding this you can begin your book on the correct path and avoid many of the pitfalls newbies make because they think they can wing it, who think their words are golden and everyone will line up to buy their precious novel, memoir, cookbook or children's book.

A high-end restaurant patron can tell if a meal is properly prepared. The diner most likely is not a gourmet chef and could not prepare the perfect entrée but they know something is wrong with the taste, texture or color of the food.

Much the same way a reader can tell by the first few pages of your book if you are a good writer. There is just something that puts them off and they move on to the next "Look Inside."

The editors and lit agents know what those turn off are and you should as well. Learn how to edit and proof your book to attract more prospective readers and turn them into buyers and fans. The first two titles help you accomplish that goal. The last one will help you market your book.

"Long live the King" hailed Entertainment Weekly upon publication of Stephen King's On Writing. Part memoir, part master class by one of the bestselling authors of all time, this superb volume is a revealing and practical view of the writer's craft, comprising the basic tools of the trade every writer must have. King's advice is grounded in his vivid memories from childhood through his emergence as a writer, from his struggling early career to his widely reported, near-fatal accident in 1999—and how the inextricable link between writing and living spurred his recovery. Brilliantly structured, friendly and inspiring, On Writing will empower and entertain everyone who reads it—fans, writers, and anyone who loves a great story well told. --Amazon.com description

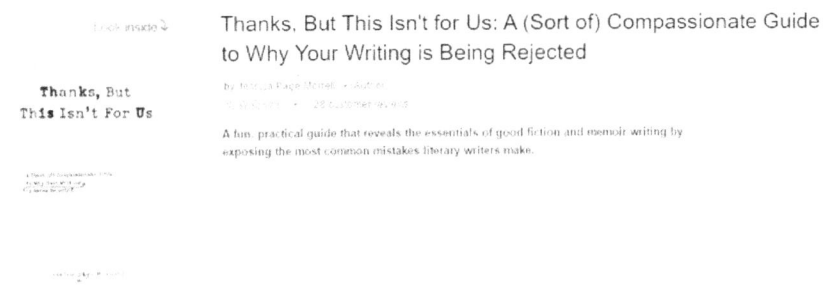

Thanks, But This Isn't for Us: A (Sort of) Compassionate Guide to Why Your Writing is Being Rejected

by Jessica Page Morrell (Author)

A fun, practical guide that reveals the essentials of good fiction and memoir writing by exposing the most common mistakes literary writers make.

All great works of fiction and memoir are unique-but most bad novels, stories, and memoirs have a lot in common.

From clunky dialogue to poorly sketched out characters, sagging pacing to exaggerated prose, these beginners' mistakes drive any agent or editor to their stock rejection letter, telling the aspiring writer "Thanks, but this isn't for us," and leaving many to wonder what exactly it is that they're doing wrong.

Veteran writing coach, developmental editor, and writing instructor Jessica Page Morrell will fill in the gaps in every rejection letter you've ever received. In Thanks, But This Isn't for Us, Morrell uses her years of experience to isolate the specific errors beginners make, including the pitfalls of unrealistic dialogue, failing to "show, not tell," and over-the-top plot twists. These are just a few of the problems that keep writers from breaking through with their work. Sympathetic and humane, but pulling no punches, Thanks, But This Isn't for Us shows writers precisely where they've gone wrong and how to get on the right track. In sixteen to-the-point chapters, with checklists, exercises, takeaway tips, and a glossary, Morrell helps readers transcend these mistakes so that they don't have to learn the hard way: with another rejection letter. – Amazon.com description

Social Media for Writers: Marketing Strategies for Building Your Audience and Selling Books
by Tee Morris (Author), Pip Ballantine (Author), Chuck Wendig (Foreword)
★★★★★ · 2 customer reviews

Look inside ↓

Kindle	Paperback	Audible	Other Sellers
$9.21	$9.99	$17.95	from $9.99

Buy new $9.99

Only 13 left in stock (more on the way)
Ships from and sold by Amazon.com. Gift-wrap available.

Want it tomorrow, June 27? Order within 6 hrs 11 mins and choose One-Day Shipping at checkout. Details.

List Price: $17.95 Save: $8.33 (49%)

40 New from $9.99

FREE Shipping on orders with at least $25 of books.

Maximize the Potential of Your Online Brand!

Over the past decade, social media has transformed from a fad into a necessity for writers. But for the inexperienced author, trying to make sense of--much less master--the available platforms can be a frustrating experience. The variety of social media options alone is dizzying enough: WordPress, Tumblr, Facebook, Twitter, Google+, YouTube, Pinterest, and more.

That's where this guide comes in. Whether you're just starting to create an audience or looking to refine your online presence, Social Media for Writers will equip you with the essential tools you'll need to succeed. In this book you'll learn how to:

Develop an editorial calendar: schedule consistent, quality content for your blog and work with other authors on guest posts and blog tours

Create an online brand: write content for several different networks, and tie them together to develop an authoritative, trusted voice

Utilize "best practices": learn the ins-and-outs of the online community and how to maximize the potential of each platform

Build a community: make connections and create a fan base to endorse your work. Amazon.com description.

Alison.com for free tutorials on MS Word

Here is a website that offers free courses in MS Word. Find the one that corresponds to the version of Word that you have. It will make your writing life easier.

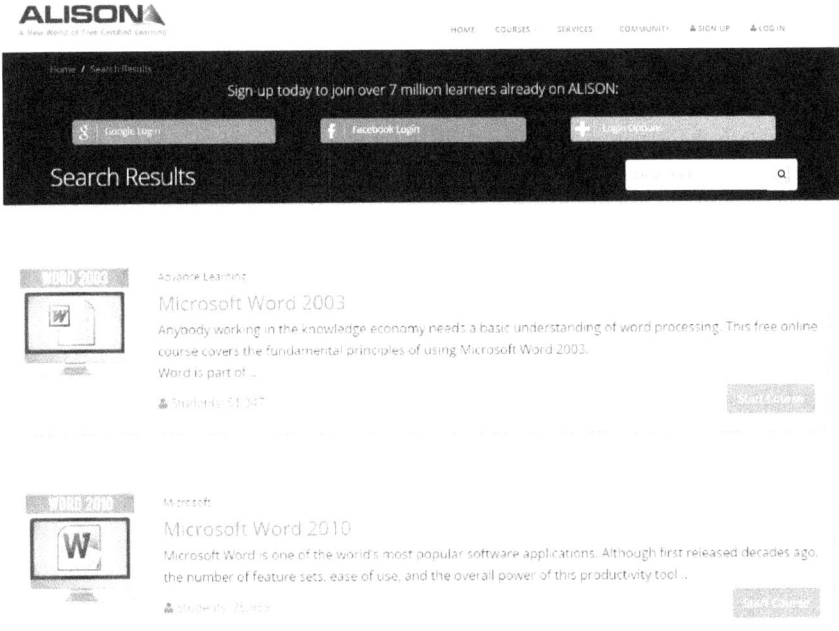

I have taken courses in Excel, Word and Photography. There are well presented and easy to follow along.

#1 Creating a professional quality book is difficult.

It is not my intent to discourage you, rather to open your eyes to the industry mysteries. Creating a piece of garbage is a snap. If you're not careful, if you don't endeavor to write a professional quality book, the readers will toss yours into the ever-growing heap of trash and you will languish in obscurity, angry at the world for not recognizing your genius.

The task of self-publishing is easy and has generated a glut of bad books. Maybe six percent are good, perhaps one percent are excellent and a handful are runaway successes.

I consider my books fair to good but not excellent. My favorite author, the late Stephen E. Ambrose, took dull, boring history and brought it to life with compelling dialogue and narration that kept me riveted to the story. *Band of Brothers*, *Nothing Like it in the World* and *Undaunted Courage* are three examples. I most likely will never reach his level but I know excellent writing when I read it. It's what I strive for every day.

The problem is many novice authors are delusional about their abilities to write. Their lack of understanding about the basic skills needed in grammar, syntax, point of view, voice, dialogue, formatting, and punctuation is mind boggling to one who has spent decades honing this craft. Even as I start my twenty-ninth book, I know there is a great deal I do not know. I constantly read advice on writing, publishing and social media. I will periodically take college level writing courses to learn what's new and to refresh my memory. It's an endless process. Yet every day, neophytes who think they have a story to tell, sit down at a keyboard and start banging away. They're unable to spot the typos, grammatical and basic punctuation errors they're making because they don't know the rules exist or at best don't think they are important. As my first writing instructor told us, "You don't know what you don't know and I'm here to teach you."

I still struggle with switching tense and the use of passive voice. I labor over each page hunting for them. I rely on MS Word's grammar and spell check, which picks up many mistakes but some still evade detection. I am aware of my issues and endeavor to find and fix them as a gardener digging crabgrass out of his lawn one blade at a time.

Naiveté is a chronic problem

It spans all aspects of the creative fields. Here are two examples.

I studied Advertising Copywriting at the School of Visual Arts in the 1970s. My instructor, Jay Michael Wolf, introduced me to the Unique Selling Proposition (USP) as developed by the Ted Bates Agency. Simply put, you find something unique about your product or service and make that the concept for your ad campaign.

An example would be:

The 2016 Chevrolet Camaro is the Motor Trend Car of the Year

That is a USP because no other car in the world can make that statement. It set's the Camaro apart from all others. Even if the competitors made a case that their car was of higher quality, ran faster, handled better they still could not make the claim for the 2016 Motor Trend Car of the Year. In 2017 the title was pass to another car.

The easiest ad you can produce is something generic, a campaign that could apply to almost any other product in the market. Think of how many products claim "New and Improved" on their labels. The advertising hacks have overused this tag line to the point it has lost all impact.

The USP concept is simple enough, but I was amazed how much bad advertising those who call themselves professionals produce every year. Quite often, the concept is the first thing that pops into their head, or worse the client's head who has zero training in advertising. What the client does have is an open checkbook and going along with the client's idea is the path of least resistance. As one frustrated Creative Director told me, "The trouble with Advertising is that everyone thinks they can do it."

If you've ever watched American Idol, you observed delusional, tone-deaf people who can't carry a tune or remember the lyrics lash out at the judges after being disqualified from competition. They believed their performance was stellar and the clueless judges couldn't appreciate their talent. As they stormed off the stage and screamed obscenities, they vowed, "I'll be back next year and then you'll be sorry."

The same mindset is rampant in writing and unlike American Idol, there are no gatekeepers to send the bad performers home with a rejection slip clutched in their fist.

As long as the writer conforms to minimum standards and avoids obscene material and plagiarism, they can publish alongside the great works of Ambrose, Steinbeck and Fitzgerald.

Factoid

Publishers won't accept unsolicited manuscripts. They want your represented by a literary agent who accepts one out of ten thousand submissions. Those are your odds.

Benefits of Traditional Publishing

A team of experts works on publishing and distributing your book. The editor and agent are professionals. They have the skills to make your book as strong as possible. Your only responsibility is writing.

Wider distribution through brick and mortar stores with a sales team to get your book on the shelf.

However, this is evolving. Publishers now expect writers to deliver completely finished work and have a social media presence.

Downside of Traditional Publishing

You need a literary agent to represent you to the publishers.

Agents really don't want newbies because of their unrealistic expectations.

If you get an agent there is no guarantee they will find you a publisher.

The time lag is at least eighteen to twenty-four months before publication.

Your book may be pulled at the last minute by marketing or sales.

One month on the bookstore shelf and you're gone if your book isn't selling.

You have no control over title, content, cover or marketing.

Benefits of Indie Publishing

You know you'll can publish as quickly or as slowly as you prefer.

You make all decisions about creating, publishing and promoting your book, so you know what's going on with every aspect of your project.

You earn higher royalties and your book will be available as long as you wish.

What is best for you, Print or Digital?

You don't know which will be the best so do both. Besides, why limit yourself?

#2 Handling criticism of your work

Last year I attended a writer's group where we shared samples of each other's work. One writer eagerly offered me a chapter of his completed novel. I read though a few pages, told him it had a good story line but I noticed an issue. He had confused "there" with "their" throughout the story. His face dropped as he asked in a tone of disbelief, "What do you mean?"

I said, "The word 'there' is used as either an adverb, a pronoun or a noun. 'Their' is a possessive pronoun. You've confused the two. As an example you wrote, 'is this there car that's parked over their.' You need to reverse the words. In addition, the sentence requires a question mark. Before I could finish, he snatched the papers from my hand. As he sulked away he said, "That's just your opinion."

Keep in mind I did not criticize his work in front of others. As the rule goes, I started with a compliment. His reaction was one of defensiveness. He was thin-skinned and incapable of hearing the slightest critique of his work. Perhaps it was the first time anyone had ever told him the truth or he was embarrassed by a simple mistake. I will never know.

All writers face criticism. It's the nature of the craft. The criticism comes from your critique group, an honest rejection letter, an enraged reader or your mother-in-law. The critics are ever present and can wreak havoc on your self-esteem.

Those who offer constructive criticism will begin with something positive and spell out their opinion on certain issues with specific examples. The critic will be respectful of the writer and never pile on by pointing out a litany of errors. All drafts have mistakes but there is no need to point each one out. That will overwhelm the writer. Rather than saying the writer made twenty-five typos in the first chapter, suggest he or she use spell check to see if there are any errors. Let the writer find out on his or her own.

Destructive criticism is toxic and offered by the critic as if theirs is the final authority. They offer no perspective and the critique is vague. The critic will dismiss the writer's work in broad terms as dreadful, terrible and the worst thing ever. The critic takes a rude or aggressive position while offering no specific examples.

If you are on the receiving end, ask yourself if the critic makes a valid point and what can you learn from it but never allow destructive criticism to get to you.

#3 What labels you an amateur

Show, don't tell

Showing means you have a character in your story experience something. Tell means you just explain what happens.

Telling Sentence: "The boat ride was harrowing," Joe said.

Showing Sentences: "White caps formed as sea spray drenched all on deck. We held tight to the railing but were unable to keep our footing. In spite of the engine running at full speed, we swept closer to the rocks that jutted out of the coastline. The fiberglass boat would not withstand a crash. A swell picked up the craft and moved us back out to sea enough for us to make a clear shot towards the dock. As we neared the shore, the engine cut out and we were once again at the mercy of the storm. Another craft neared and tossed us a towline and we were able to dock and tie off. My legs wobbled as I climbed on to the deck. It was my last boat ride for some time," Joe said

Which example gave you a feel for the experience?

Consistent Point of View (POV)

Source: http://www.lbcc.edu/WRSC/documents/BeingConsistent_POV.pdf

Point of view is the perspective from which a sentence or paragraph is written.

Always use the same person or personal pronoun throughout a story

1. First person point of view uses the pronouns "I" and "we".

Example: "I ran like I was chased by a bear."

2. Second person point of view uses the pronoun "you".

Example: "You can't see the game from the nose bleed section of this stadium."

3. Third person point of view uses the pronouns "he", "she", "it", "they" or a character's name.

Example: "Al Pacino is a gifted actor. His roles are convincing and you never think of his earlier pictures."

Avoid confusing shifts

A shift from one point of view to another or "Head Hopping" will tear a reader out of your story.

Example: "Independent <u>writers</u> quickly learn that <u>you</u> are on <u>your</u> own for editing and marketing."

The writer shifted from the third person (<u>writers</u>) to the second person (<u>you</u> and <u>your</u>).

Correct: "Independent <u>writers</u> quickly learn that <u>they</u> are on <u>their</u> own for editing and marketing."

Inconsistent in noun vs pronoun

Be consistent in using the right singular or plural pronoun. If the noun that the pronoun refers to is singular, use the singular pronoun for that person. If the noun is plural, use the plural pronoun.

Incorrect: <u>An Indie Writer</u> should proofread <u>their</u> books.

Correct: <u>An Indie Writer</u> proofreads <u>his or her</u> books only after it is complete

Never shortchange your readers.

Tie up loose ends before the story ends.

If there is a murder – reveal the killer at the end.

A Romance should have a happy ending, with the exception of

Romeo and Juliet, as one of my writers pointed out.

The lost child is rescued.

"To be continued" may work in a weekly TV series but not in books.

Use of !!!!!!!!!

Editors, professional writers and Literary Agents see exclamation points as the sign of a lazy writer, or worse–an amateur. While grammatically correct, the rationale is those judging your work will see them in a negative light.

F. Scott Fitzgerald said it best: "An exclamation mark is like laughing at your own joke

Instead of: "I'm giving you one last chance!"

Consider: "This is your last chance."

THE USE OF MULTIPLE EXCLAMATION POINTS, ALL CAPS AND BOLD FONT IS A DEAD GIVEAWAY THAT YOU HAVE NO IDEA WHAT YOU ARE DOING !!!!!!!!!!

If you need gimmicks to make your readers pay attention, there is something wrong with your story telling.

Overuse of first names in dialogue

"Hey Joe, I was wondering if we could score tickets to tonight's game? Now Joe, remember I got them last time so I need you, Joe, to handle this today. And remember Joe, I like an aisle seat close to the concession stand. What do you say, Joe?" Bill asked.

Consider: "Hey Joe, I was wondering if we could score tickets to tonight's game? Now remember I got them last time so I need you to handle this today. And remember, I like an aisle seat close to the concession stand. What do you say?" Bill asked.

#4 Ban these words from your books
These words label you as a novice writer.

That

Then

So

Very

Suddenly

Is and all of its variations

Started

Examples: <u>So</u> Bennie <u>suddenly</u> ran <u>very</u> fast into the room.

Avoid sentences beginning with "well" or "so." It's common in real life but it's annoying in a book. This helps you clean up your writing to make it effortless to the reader.

"Sudden" means quickly and without warning.

"Very" means in a high degree; extremely; exceedingly.

Consider: Bennie ran into the room.

There are no degrees of fast. No sort of fast, kind of fast, really really fast. Fast is fast. Yes, something may be faster.

Replace the boring verb "ran."

Consider: Bennie jogged into the room

Replace the boring noun "room."

Consider: Bennie jogged into the kitchen.

Omit "That"

The word "that" can often be omitted.

Example: "There's not much <u>that</u> this chef can't cook."

Consider: "There's not much this chef can't cook."

Example: We use the word <u>that</u> in sentences often, <u>that</u> it's something <u>that</u> I think <u>that</u> we might want to stop. Stop <u>that</u>. Try dropping the word <u>that</u> and you'll notice <u>that</u> your sentences are tighter.

Consider: We use the word "that" in sentences often, it's something I think we might want to stop. Try dropping the word and you'll notice your sentences are tighter.

Omit "Then"

"Then" points vaguely to the existing timeline after that last thing you talked about. The new action taking place in a subsequent sentence already implies it. You can often eliminate your thens without disrupting meaning or flow.

Example: I woke up, <u>then</u> I, brushed my teeth, <u>then</u> I, combed my hair, <u>then</u> I went to work.

Consider: I woke up, brushed my teeth, combed my hair and went to work.

Eliminate "In order to"

A self-evident statement which slows the reader down.

Example: We're removing your appendix <u>in order to</u> save your life.

Consider: We're removing your appendix to save your life.

All forms of "Is"

Is, am, are, was, or were—whatever form your "is" takes, it's likely useless.

Example: I <u>was</u> driving the car.

Consider: I drove the car.

Note how I changed present tense driving to past tense drove.

There are exceptions: If the description is about a state of being: we <u>are</u> here or they <u>are</u> in a race.

Started

"I <u>started</u> taking French lessons last year," implies I'm still taking them today. If I stopped after one class then I'd write, "I <u>took</u> French lessons last year."

He <u>started</u> singing. If he stopped after a single song, use "He sang."

If you are telling us his singing will be background noise for a while, write: He <u>started</u> singing and never shut up.

In MS Word, highlight and right mouse click a word to find synonyms you can use. Highlight one of the suggested replacements, click on it and MS Word will automatically insert that word instead. If you're not happy with the choices, click on Thesaurus for more options.

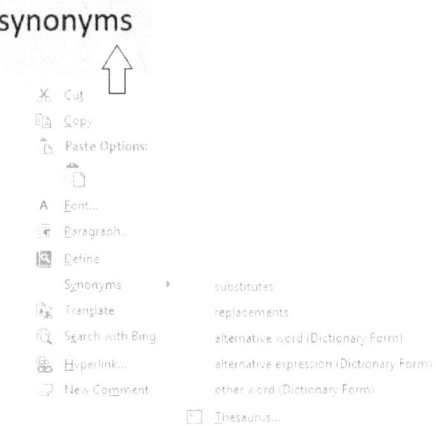

Words have their own personal territory about 10 words apart. Don't invade it.

There is a time and place for repeating words for experienced writers, but in general, it's bad form to overuse a word, especially within a small body of text.

Actual example:

She stepped out onto the street, looked about, and purposely strode in the direction of Booth Street, weaving in and out of street vendors, street cars and less savory characters. A street sweeper glided down the street weaving in and out of parked cars. As she approached Booth Street, the street sweeper glided too close to her knocking her out onto the street.

Read the above paragraph out loud and stress each underlined word. Count the number of times each of those words are used.

Now rewrite the paragraph, eliminating the repetition, to make it read faster and smoother:

_____

_____

_____

_____

_____

_____

_____

Mix Proper Nouns with Pronouns

Definition: A pronoun (I, me, he, she, herself, you, it, that, they, each, few, many, who, whoever, whose, someone, everybody, etc.) is a word that takes the place of a noun. In the sentence Joe saw Jill, and he waved at her, the pronouns he and her take the place of Joe and Jill, respectively. There are three types of pronouns: subject (for example, he); object (him); or possessive (his). OnlineDictionary

Example: Katie strolled down the street, enjoying her day off. The tantalizing scent of peach pie drew Katie into the corner café.

Minutes later Katie sank her fork into the flaky crust, savored the sweetness of the fruity filling, and asked herself why it had taken her ages to indulge in her favorite dessert.

Consider using the proper noun once in the beginning to establish the character and then pronouns until you introduce a new character: Katie strolled down the street, enjoying her day off. The tantalizing scent of peach pie drew her into the corner café.

Minutes later she sank her fork into the flaky crust and savored the sweetness of the fruity filling. Why had it had taken her ages to indulge in her favorite dessert?

Avoid repeating the same syntax

Subject + Verb+ Object.

It's boring.

Example: I drove to the Deli. I bought some beer. I went home. The game was on. I sat down. I fell asleep. I woke up. My team won.

Rewrite the paragraph to make it exciting and free flowing.

_____

_____

_____

Tighten up your Prose

Let's look at two common amateur errors, the use of up and down. The direction is implied and the prepositions "up" and "down" is redundant.

Robert climbed <u>up</u> the ladder to change the light bulb, slipped and fell <u>down</u> onto the pavement.

The reader can figure out the directions he was moving when he climbed and when he fell. The use of up and down is redundant and slows the reader.

Ban Adjectives and Adverbs from your work

An **adjective** is a word that modifies a noun (or pronoun) to make it more specific: a "rotten" egg, a "cloudy" day, a "lovely" lady, or a "tall," "cool" glass of water. Source: Vocabulary.com

An **adverb** is a word that modifies anything other than a noun, usually a verb. If you listen patiently to my grammar lesson, you will learn that patiently is an adverb in this sentence.

Many adverbs end in –ly, like quickly, happily, or grudgingly. Sometimes adverbs are harder to spot. If I ask you to talk very loudly, then very is the adverb: it describes how you are supposed to talk. - Source: Vocabulary.com

Nothing screams hack writer more than gumming up a novel with adverbs and adjectives.

The hallmark of inexperienced writers is to throw in expressive words to make their prose melodramatic. Such cosmetic touch-up often turns out to be boring. Adverbs like "tenderly" or "quickly" or "hastily." point to an emotion or movement, yet don't they offer effect. No matter how much icing you put on an over-baked cake, it will still be over baked.

Example: He spoke to her tenderly as they hugged.

Consider: He spoke to her as they hugged.

Assignment: Rewrite these sentences and rid them of adverbs and adjectives. (don't forget "so")

The moon was so beautiful tonight, lighting up the fragrant, wet, green foliage so that it practically glowed, casting a bright, white, translucent shadow across all the crisp, straight lines surrounding me as I stood within the wonderful woods I have always loved.

There are two basic types of adjectives, broad and specific. Broad: beautiful, wonderful. Specific: wet, green, bright, white, translucent, crisp, straight

_____

_____

_____

The very loud train pulled into the darkened station that had been littered with trash from an earlier rousing football tailgate party. The smell of stank beer, over cooked hot dogs and ample amounts of relish filled the air as if it were a dank, moldy overcoat.

_____

_____

_____

Additional Resource: *Tips that will improve your fiction writing and make your manuscript memorable- https://www.scribendi.com*

Example: Carrying a <u>steaming</u> and <u>fragrant</u> mug, she walked <u>angrily</u> and <u>loudly</u> into his office.

Why write that, when you could have simply said: Carrying her peppermint tea, she stormed into his office.

The second sentence actually gives the reader more information using fewer words.

Mark Twain had it right: "As to the Adjective: when in doubt, strike it out."

Stephen King wrote, "The adverb is not your friend."

"With adverbs, the writer usually tells us he or she is afraid he/she isn't expressing himself/herself clearly, that he or she is not getting the point or the picture across."

From http://theeditorsblog.net/

"Definitely restrict their (adverbs) use in dialogue tags. (he said – she said) Yes, adverbs were once quite popular as modifiers for the verbs in dialogue tags. But they aren't popular for that purpose today. Adverbs paired with creative dialogue tags can come across as melodramatic or as amateurish storytelling. As the work of an inexperienced author."

These tags look ridiculous:

"You can't have any more," he hissed.

"Run away," she said evasively.

"I'll throw a pie in your face," she said jokingly.

Just use he said, she said.

Don't insult your readers. They aren't as stupid as you think.

A fellow writer in my group had written a novel where he used the name Ernest Hemingway in dialogue. He felt it necessary to follow it with the explanation "a famous writer." What reader of adult fiction does not know of Ernest Hemingway? You insult you're readers intelligence if you see the need to spell everything out to them. This is a turn off.

Here is an example, exaggerated to make my point:

My grandfather, who is related to me, once met Babe Ruth, a famous baseball player at Yankee Stadium, where baseball games are played. He talked to "the Babe," Babe Ruth's nickname, about the next game to be held in Boston, a large town in Massachusetts that is located on the east coast of the United States. The Babe was confident they would beat the Red Sox, the name of the Boston team in the double header, where two games are played back to back.

My favorite: "He slammed the door loudly." Thanks for spelling it out. I'm stupid enough to think he slammed it quietly.

#5 Proper punctuation of dialogue

Dialogue punctuation has its own rules. Commas go in particular places, as do terminal marks such as periods and question marks.

The only thing between quote marks are the spoken words and punctuation. Other parts of the same sentence—dialogue tags and action or thought—go outside the quotation marks.

Example: "Everyone, get your luggage off of the cart now," he said

These spoken words go inside the quote marks while <u>he said</u> goes outside.

Dialogue begins with a capitalized word, no matter where in the sentence it begins.

Examples:

1.) "Get me the book now," Frank said.

2.) Frank ran up to the librarian and said, "Get the book now."

If the dialogue is interrupted, it is not capped when resumed.

Example: Frank ran up to the librarian and said, "Get me the book now," as he slapped the table, "my bus is here."

Only direct dialogue requires quote marks. Indirect dialogue is a report that someone spoke.

Direct: "She was a bore," he said.

Indirect: "George told me 'she was a bore.' No wonder he didn't go out with her," he said.

Begin dialogue with a capitalized word, no matter where in the sentence it begins

Example: "Hello everyone."

A single line of dialogue with no dialogue tag. It is used when the conversation is between two people and the reader knows which is speaking.

Example: "He wrote to you."

When the tag <u>she said</u> is part of the same sentence, it is not capped.

Correct: "He wrote to you," she said.

Incorrect: "He wrote to you," She said.

When a dialogue tag starts the sentence, it is followed by a comma before the quote mark. The period or question mark that ends the sentence falls inside the quote marks.

Example: She said, "Let's leave now."

Single line of dialogue with dialogue tag and action.

As always, enclosed the dialogue in quotes followed by a comma. The dialogue is placed before the closing quotation mark.

"Her perfume stank up the car," he said, hoping Rachael didn't hear the complaint.

Dialogue punctuation worksheet

Assignment: Insert quote marks and commas in the proper place

Take the train to town It's faster

She called you Randy said but you didn't care

He called you (a question)

He called you Brenda asked the loathing clear in her voice and posture

He called you Francis said

Anna said Let's leave now

Bill called you Dorothy said hoping Brenda didn't hear her

Walking towards Steven she said He called you

Frankie called you Jose said but you let it go to voicemail

Tony called you Amy said hoping to provoke anger But you let it go to voicemail

Answer Key page: 87

#6 The good news - Indie Publishing is easy
The bad news is everyone is doing it and there are no filters.

Online booksellers are not in business to judge the quality of your work. Their business model is to sell books and make money for their stockholders and owners.

They don't care whether they're selling well-written, thoroughly edited pieces of literature, or garbage that some marginally literate, delusional goofball who thinks he's the next F. Scott Fitzgerald threw up on his keyboard.

Following is dialogue from an Indie writer:

"Waste time not in intoxicating stony silence whilst allowing the deep dark red lifeblood that abscesses in my copious veins to ooze through cavities of unrestrained desire and dribble down to inundate me with its cerise shade as if it were a waterfall in some remote South American jungle teaming with piranha fishes."

This is your competition along with Charles Dickens and J.K Rowling. Where do you fit in?

Assignment: Rewrite the paragraph to make it readable

_____

_____

_____

_____

_____

#7 The odds are against you
but keep writing, publishing, studying and marketing.

The Writer's Odds

http://williamdietrich.com/the-writers-odds/

by BDIETRICH on MARCH 4, 2013

Thriller author James Patterson made $94 million in 2012, according to Forbes. He's one of 145,900 American "writers and authors" counted by the Bureau of Labor Statistics, a quarter of them part-time, two-thirds of them self-employed, and with median earnings of $55,420.

Pollsters report more than 80 percent of Americans would like to be author, and in 2011 statisticians counted 329,259 books published in the United States, and 2.2 million books published in the world. Google estimates 130 million books have been published in human history.

Yet there is a place for you in publishing and you should always have a project in the works.

#8 Romantic Novels lead the sales categories
Yet How To books and Self Help sell the most.

Although the number of romantic books available out numbers the How To and Self Help books. The later has a higher sales volume.

Romance, science fiction, and fantasy books are the best suited for self-publishing. In fact, half of the e-book bestsellers in the romance, science fiction, and fantasy genres on Amazon are self-published.
Source: http://selfpublishingrelief.com/self-published-genres-sell-most/

Nonfiction with a popular topic does well. Religious books are a perfect case in point.

And with fiction, some genres do better than others. Indie romance/erotica novels, for instance, have thrived in the e-book arena.

Visit the bestseller book list on Amazon.com. In the left column are the genres. Click on each one to see what is selling best. Find the one you wish to write in and see what works. Remember, you want to emulate success not plagiarize it.

https://www.amazon.com/best-sellers-books-Amazon/zgbs/books/ref=zg_bs_nav_0

#9 Your title needs to be unique

Don't be a copycat that can be confused with other titles.

Apparently this is a real problem for navigators.

5.0 out of 5 stars **Reads like a whodunnit!**

By Fitz on December 21, 2010

I bought How to Avoid Huge Ships as a companion to Captain Trimmer's other excellent titles: How to Avoid a Train, and How to Avoid the Empire State Building. These books are fast paced, well written and the hard won knowledge found in them is as inspirational as it is informational. After reading them I haven't been hit by anything bigger than a diesel bus. Thanks captain!

Book Description. *Warning: This book may cause flatulence.* Walter is a fine dog, except for one small problem: he has gas. He can't help it; it's just the way he is. Fortunately, the kids Billy and Betty love him regardless, but Father says he's got to go! Poor Walter, he's going to the dog pound tomorrow. And then, in the night, burglars strike. Walter has his chance to be a hero. A children's beloved classic, this story will have kids rolling on the floor with laughter. Adults are permitted to laugh too.

Does your title accurately describe your book?

#10 What sells as an eBook
may not sell in print

And what sells in print may not sell in eBooks. Since you can't know
which will be best – do both.

eReaders and tablets are here to stay, but according to a 2014 study
only 4% of active readers are reading digital books exclusively. That
means 96% of readers still buy printed books. Even among a younger
demographic (age 30 and below), 50% of readers are purchasing
printed books ONLY.

As a self-published print author you need to make your book
available as an eBook as well. You receive unlimited shelf-space,
worldwide distribution, low or no manufacturing costs per unit and
nearly instant delivery to your readers.

Source: http://bookarma.net/blog/eBook-vs-print-book/

#11 Build your Social Media NOW Not Later
Using Facebook, Twitter and Pinterest to sell books

Start with a special group

https://www.facebook.com/groups/729019770514057/

Begin by posting your future story and inviting feedback.

There are many books out there on Social Media, but I found this one to be informative, complete and well written for the social media novice like me.

Social Media for Writers: Marketing Strategies for Building Your Audience and Selling Books

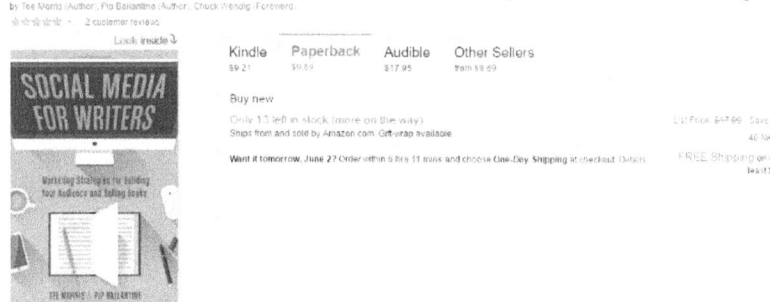

Additional Resources

From Inc. Magazine

http://www.inc.com/the-muse/how-to-build-a-killer-social-media-presence.html

60 Awesome Social-Media Tools for Entrepreneurs

http://www.inc.com/jeff-haden/60-awesome-social-media-tools-for-entrepreneurs.html

DASHBOARDS & MANAGEMENT TOOLS

1. SocialBro

Our Listening and Audience Intelligence gives you the information needed to drive your social strategy

Uncover and track the quality of your audience

Understand crossover between communities

Combine content with relationship analysis

2. Tweetdeck

TweetDeck is a social media dashboard application for management of Twitter accounts. Like other Twitter applications it interfaces with the Twitter API to allow users to send and receive tweets and view profiles.-Wikipedia

#12 Write a Great Description like the Pros

Consider these TV show descriptions written by pros. You may ask, "But I'm writing a book not a TV program, how does this apply to me?" A quality description is a good model to emulate no matter what the media.

—— "Conviction," ABC. A lawyer and former first daughter (Hayley Atwell) takes a job with the New York district attorney's office to avoid jail time for drugs and political damage for her mother's Senate campaign. (30 words)

—— "Notorious," ABC. A provocative look at the sexy and dangerous interplay of criminal law and the media. (12 words)

—— "Imaginary Mary," ABC. Jenna Elfman plays a fiercely independent career woman whose life is turned upside down when she meets the love of her life — a divorced father with three kids. (26 words)

— "Downward Dog," ABC. Based on the web series, the comedy looks at the life of a struggling millennial (Allison Tolman) from the perspective of her philosophical dog, Martin. (26 words)

Harry Potter and the Cursed Child-Parts 1 & 2

Based on an original new story by J.K. Rowling, Jack Thorne and John Tiffany, the Cursed Child is the eighth story in the Harry Potter series and the first official Harry Potter story to be presented on stage. The play will receive its world premiere in London's West End on July 30, 2016.

It was always difficult being Harry Potter and it isn't much easier now that he is an overworked employee of the Ministry of Magic, a husband and father of three school-age children.

While Harry grapples with a past that refuses to stay where it belongs, his youngest son Albus must struggle with the weight of a family legacy he never wanted. As past and present fuse ominously, both father and son learn the uncomfortable truth: sometimes, darkness comes from unexpected places.

(134 Words)

Assignment:

Write your book description. Even if you haven't started writing your novel, how to or memoir, start on the description now. It can evolve along with your story. By the time you're ready to publish, this key element will be ready.

Your Book Description should be about 140 words.

_____

_____

_____

_____

_____

_____

_____

_____

_____

#13 Never pay for book reviews

Publishing expert Jane Friedman writes on her blog, "Paying for professional book reviews is a controversial topic that very few authors have practical, unbiased information about. It's not even well-known in the author community that paid book reviews exist, and even less is known about the value of such reviews."
Source: https://janefriedman.com/paid-book-reviews/

Early on in the self-publishing universe, authors discovered they could pay others to post reviews of their books for a fee. It was effective at the start but soon gained a reputation bordering on fraud. I say this because the reviews reportedly were not reading the books, just synopsis or in some cases reviews written by the author and spoon-fed to the reviewer.

Amazon has sued members of a popular website who sold positive book reviews for a small fee. Amazon removed the phony reviews website and may have gone after the authors who paid for them.

Reviews may or may not help your sales. As of today, June 25, 2016 the number one best seller in print, Harry Potter and the Cursed Child - Parts One & Two has no reviews. Yet the number 100 title, a spiritual book, has over 4,000 positive reviews.

My study guides are consistently in the top 10 for Citizenship yet have only a handful of reviews.

Another thing to consider is Amazon's policy of removing reviews of your book if the reviewer is connected to you by social media. Exactly how they do this is a source of controversy. As a result, none of my friends on Facebook can post a review

#14 Make the most out of your Amazon page

If you go to Amazon.com and search Mike Swedenberg in books, you'll see a link to my author's page. There you can read about my books and view my videos. This is an excellent place for you to start marketing yourself.

This profile page allows you to add your twitter feed and your blog. Update will appear here keeping your page relevant.

Write your Bio now – not later

Time Frame that is relevant to this book: Mike Swedenberg has been self-publishing books for over four years.

Services I offer: He provides copywriting, coaching and teaches continuing education classes at Nassau Community College.

My education: His educational background in business, sales, creative writing and marketing has given him a broad base from which to approach many topics.

Validation: His writing skills is confirmed independently on Amazon.com He especially enjoys producing study guides and self-help books.

You may learn more about him at his Pinterest account https://www.pinterest.com/mikeswedenberg/

Reference: Sam Chinkes, Sound advertising, Las Vegas, NV.

Your bio should be keyed towards the book you are working on and modified for other publications in the future. As an example, the bio for my Study Guides is different than the one for my Advertising Copywriting manual.

Search Amazon's bestseller list by genre and find bios from traditional publishers you can study for format, style and length. Look for key words and phrases.

Write your Bio

#15 Pricing is Critical

What's the best price for a self-published eBook? $3.99, Smashwords research suggests.

Most authors price at $2.99…

Smashwords founder and CEO Mark Coker found that eBook authors chose to price at $2.99 "more frequently than any other price point. In last year's survey, $.99 was a more common price point than $2.99. In this year's survey, $2.99 was [chosen] about 60 percent more often."

…but $3.99 sells the most copies.

Print is different. Createspace will determine the lowest price allowed based on the size and number of pages and color interior. What you should do is check the top sellers in your genre to see what the competition is charging and price your book accordingly.

Based on the Createspace criteria, the minimum price I can set is $5.38

I set the price for the English /Spanish version at $9.95 and it outsells the others priced two dollars less on a consistent basis. All other languages in my series are priced at $7.95 and are in the top forty.

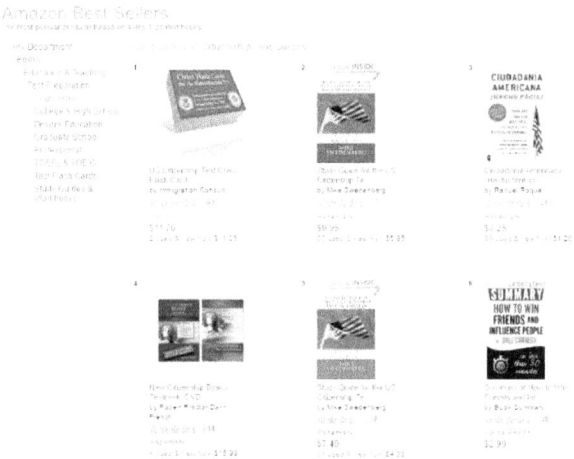

My novel, *A New York Wedding*, is at a price disadvantage. The novel is 462 pages and therefore the minimum price allowed is $15.98. Most of my competition is priced around $9.95. The only way I can make this book competitive is to reduce the number of pages by half. I believe it would detract too much from the storyline. On occasion, Amazon will offer ANYW at $14.11 with Prime's free shipping.

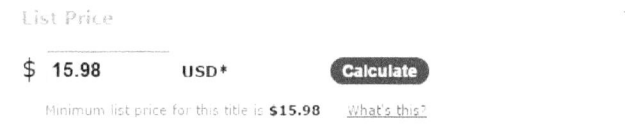

Keep this in mind when writing and editing your book. A rough estimate would be about five cents per page.

#16 Fiverr.com for reasonably priced help

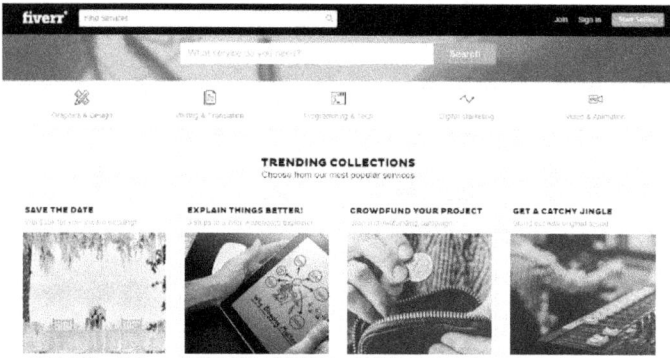

Fiverr is a global online marketplace offering tasks and services, starting at a cost of $5 per job performed, from which it gets its name. The site is primarily used by freelancers who use Fiverr to offer services to customers worldwide. -- Wikipedia

I have used Fiverr for creating my videos. The turnaround time was fast and the price was inexpensive as opposed to using a studio or agency. I don't know where else I could have produced a three minute video for $40. Was it as slick as one created by a traditional publisher? No, but it is acceptable for my purposes. As I gain experience in working with the Fiverr vendors, the videos will improve.

My other option is to spend hundreds on video software and equipment and go through a learning curve to produce my own. Since my goal is to write, publish and promote my books, homemade video production is not an option.

Visit https://www.fiverr.com/categories for a complete list of their services.

#17 A Great Book Cover won't guarantee sales but a bad one will kill it.

EBook covers and print covers are different. The eBook cover is just the front cover. Print book cover files include the back cover, front cover and spine. The dimensions of the print book cover will be different for every book–they're calculated based on how many pages there are in your book and the trim size you've chosen.

Check Amazon.com and the New York Times Best Seller List to see what the latest trends are for your genre. Use them as a guide when designing your own.

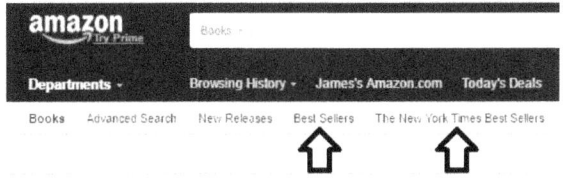

One of many sites to help you:

http://www.hongkiat.com/blog/designing-book-covers/

It is commonplace among designers and authors to share book covers for feedback before they go to publishing. Take a look at how book cover designs come to be.

Designing a concept

Book cover design tips

Book cover design tutorials

Sources for ideas

Here is a professionally designed book cover. Note the clean design and how the author's name are predominate. One font is used in only two colors.

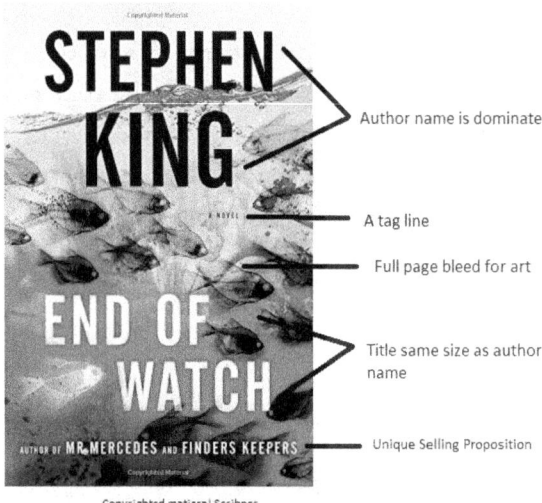

Author name is dominate

A tag line

Full page bleed for art

Title same size as author name

Unique Selling Proposition

Copyrighted matieral Scribner

A Unique Selling Proposition (USP) is a one liner to attract your attention and make cover stand out from all the rest. Only Stephen King can claim to be the author of *Mr Mercedes* and *Finders Keepers*.

A tag line tells you something about the book. In this case, it's a novel.

Other noteworthy tag lines:

Jaws -- Don't go in the water

Aliens -- In space, no one can hear you scream.

Bully Boss – Based on actual events

Think about a tag line and USP for your book?

#18 It Takes Time
Maxima enim, patientia virtus

1. My eBook sales averaged a few copies a month in 2014.

2. When I expanded to Createspace, they jumped to about 25 copies a month.

3. When I added Social Media, they jumped to about 200 a month.

4. When I changed my Search Engine Optimization (SEO) key words, I jumped to 400 copies a month by May 2016.

I's an ever evolving and moving target. You just can't hit the PUBLISH button and forget about it.

- Stephen King's first novel, Carrie, was rejected 30 times. He tossed it in the wastebasket but his wife fished it out. He earned $39 million in 2012.

- John Grisham's first novel, A Time to Kill, was rejected 12 times, and he unsuccessfully tried to sell copies from the trunk of his car. He earned $26 million last year.

- Judy Blume, who has sold 80 million books, got nothing but rejections for two straight years.

- Steve Berry, 10 million books, collected 85 rejections over 12 years before breaking through.

#19 Show/Hide is Your Friend

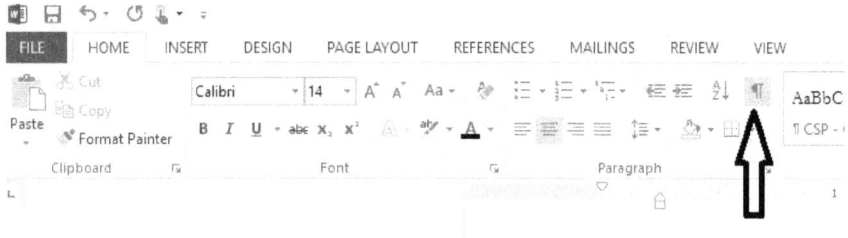

When I first noticed Show/Hide in MS Word, it was an accident. I didn't know what it was nor how to disable it. Since I didn't know what it was called, it took forever to discover the explanation. I knew if I printed my document the symbols displayed on screen would not print, but I found them annoying. It was not till I took a tutorial some years later that I discovered the power and value of the function. Using it will help you format your print books and is critical in eBooks since tab keys, use of the space bar to center lines and others is strictly forbidden.

Under the FILE tab in MS Word, Click on OPTIONS and then DISPLAY.
Make sure the boxes are checked. This will display the coding. As a
reminder, it is not important in Createspace for Print but is critical in
Smashwords eBooks.

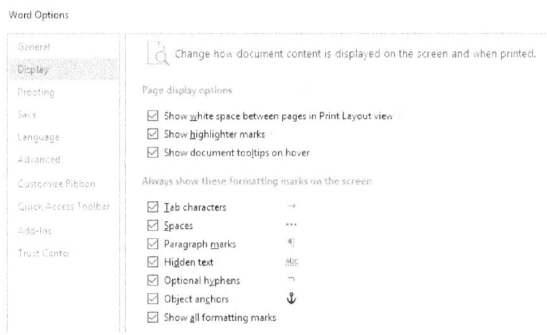

Show Hide reveals the page coding. The Section Break is forcing the second page of my Table of Contents to be centered instead of flush top as in the first page.

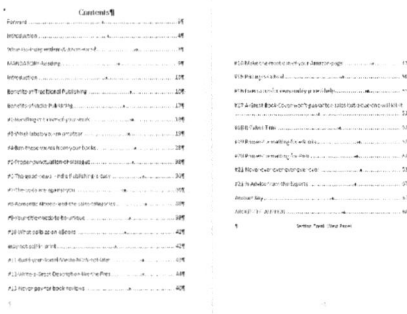

After removing Section Break, note how the page is aligned properly at the top.

#20 Proper Formatting
For Print and eBooks

Start writing your book in the proper format for which it will be published. Do it correctly from the start and you will avoid the torture of a massive editing chore at the end.

For Createspace use this link to download a formatted template. Start with 6 x 9, which is the most popular. Don't guess at the correct size. Do some research in your genre.
https://forums.createspace.com/en/community/docs/DOC-1323

EBook and Smashwords Format Rules taken in part from their website and Style Guide

Start with a .doc file maximum size 5 MB This file should be "clean" - never worked on in other word processors. This is critical since using different versions of Word on other computers can corrupt your formatting. Make a back-up copy of it before you start formatting.

Save **ONLY** in MS 97 – 2003 Document. When you SAVE your document for the first time or whenever you SAVE AS you get these options:

When you are ready to publish on Createspace, you may upload your book as a PDF. This locks in your positioning and formatting. You cannot do that with Smashwords, which requires Word 97-2003.

Open Source is another option but Smashwords does not support it.

Always use Show/Hide feature. (The backward P)

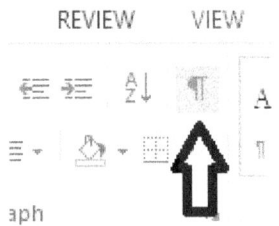

Turn off Auto Correct - Tools - AutoCorrect - AutoFormat As You Type - uncheck all but smart quotes. (Curly quotes vs, straight quotes) AutoFormat tab - uncheck the four boxes under Apply. Auto Correct can play havoc on your dialogue.

1. Click the **File** tab.
2. Click **Options**.
3. Click **Proofing**.
    If you are using Outlook, click **Mail**, and then click **Spelling and AutoCorrect**.
4. Click **AutoCorrect Options**.
5. On the **AutoCorrect** tab, make sure the **Replace text as you type** check box is NOT selected.

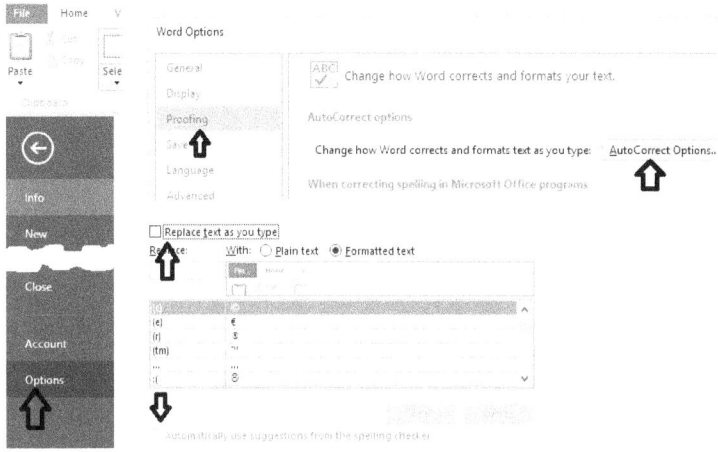

For eBooks, remove Headers, Footers, and Page Numbering. In Print, they are needed. See the headers for this book on the top including the title and my name then the page numbers on the bottom of the page centered.

Fonts Use Garamond, Arial, or Times New Roman No drop caps to begin chapters but you can make the first letter a larger font and bold. (I've had issues with this suggestion) Use 12 point for body and 14 for title. This book employs the Garamond font.

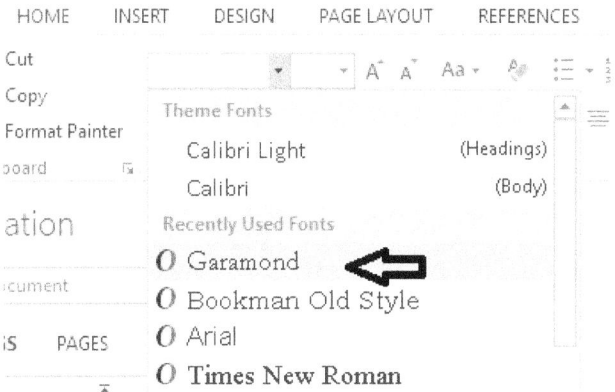

In an eBook Italics and underlining convert well, but avoid symbols (including the copyright symbol - write the word) They are fine for print.

Title and Copyright page. Here is an example of both:

Adventures of Sparky

The Search for the Butterfly Tattoo

Copyright © 2014 by Ira Levofsky

Published by Smashwords.com

All rights reserved. No part of this publication may be reproduced, distributed, or transmitted in any form or by any means, including photocopying, recording, or other electronic or mechanical methods, without the prior written permission of the publisher, except in the case of brief quotations embodied in critical reviews and certain other noncommercial uses permitted by copyright law. For permission requests, write to the Author, addressed "Attention: Permissions Coordinator," at sales@roksci.com

REMEMBER you must remove any reference to Smashwords for the Amazon upload.

Images- If you have images saved on your computer, they should be embedded in your Word file with the Insert - Picture - As File option.

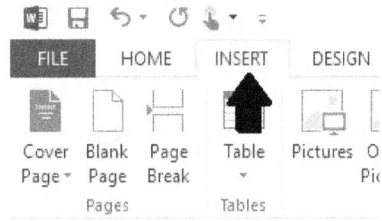

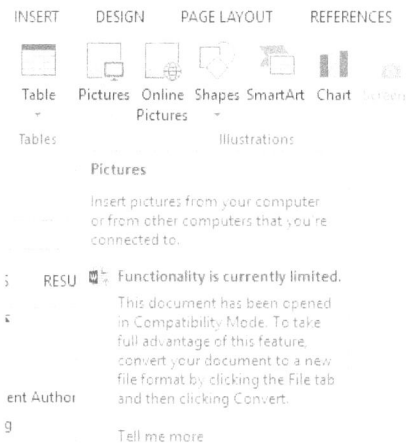

The image can be scaled by hovering the mouse on the corner of the image and dragging it diagonally to reduce the size.

Styles- Start with everything in normal style. Found at the top of the Word screen. In Word, a style is a collection of formatting instructions used to format the paragraphs in your document. Use the "Title" style for your title, "Body Text" style for body text and "Heading 1" for major headings.

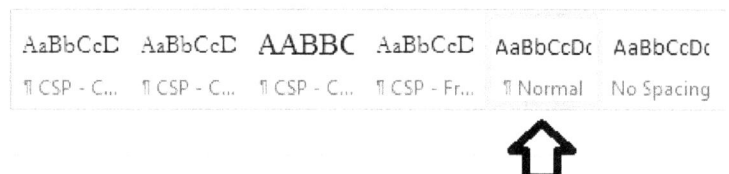

Right click on the Normal button (or any other one you choose) and click on Modify

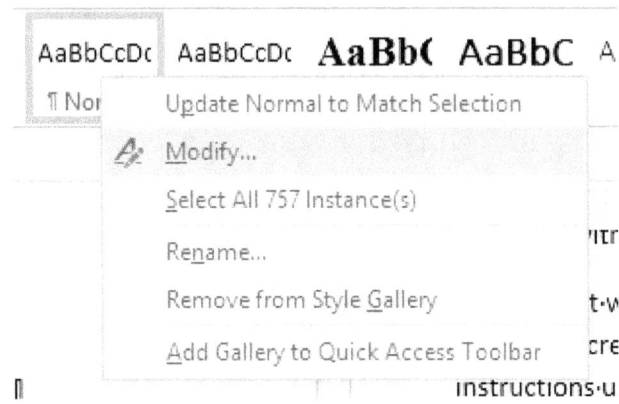

You will see a new pop up screen that allows you to modify that style for everything you do in this document. Once you make the changes in formatting, click on OK. This ensures consistency and will save you untold time and effort.

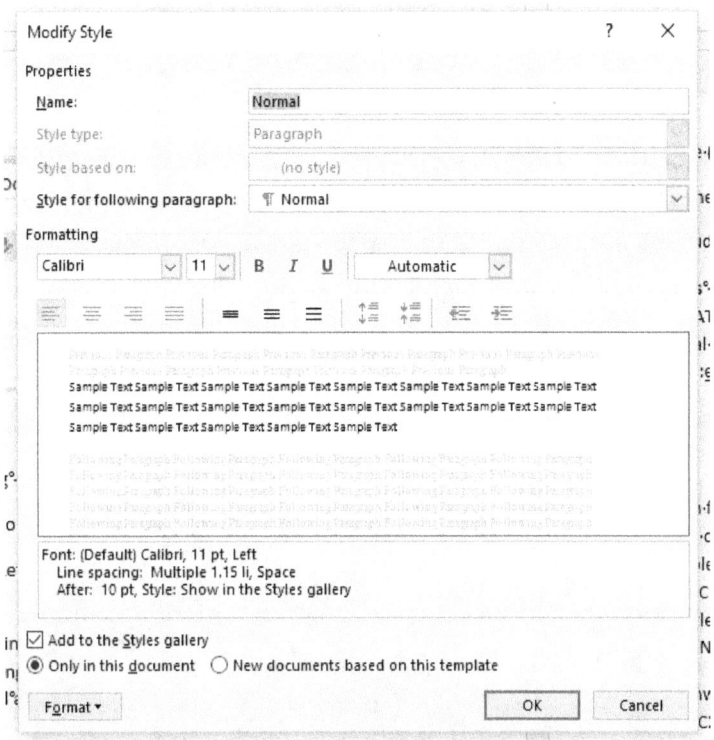

Now when you type a new chapter title, you highlight the title and click on Heading 1. Not only will your headings be consistent, you will be able to create a great Table of Contents with no effort.

On the HOME tab click on the small arrow un the Paragraph section

This will reveal a new pop up window where you can set the parameters for your style.

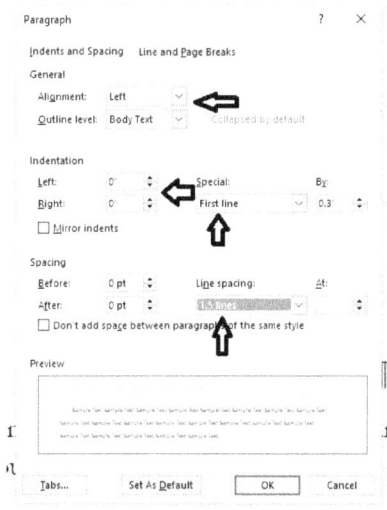

Indent – Set the left and right at 0'. Under Special, the first line should be set at .25" or .3"

Line spacing - No spaces before or after paragraphs. Use single line or 1.5 spacing.

Finally click on Set as Default and choose to keep these setting for This document only or All documents based on the Normal template. Since you'll be creating other documents with Word that require different settings, I suggest you choose this document only.

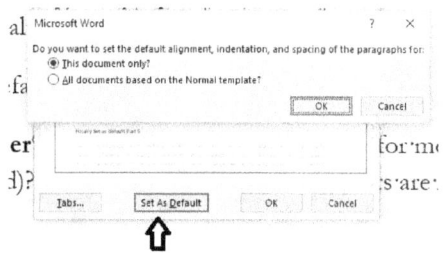

Margins- Under the Page Layout Tab, select Margins. This will reveal several options. Use Office default of Top and Bottom - 1" and Left and Right - 1.25"

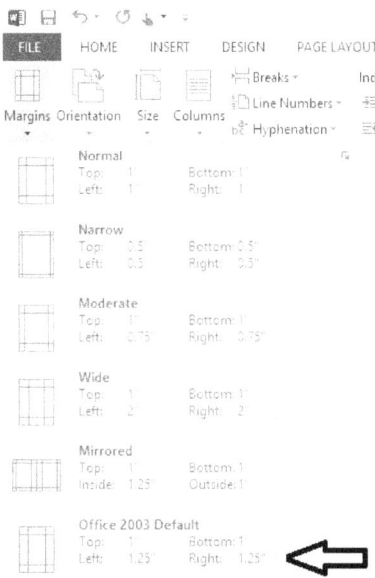

Never insert more than 4 paragraph returns - likely to create blank page. I only use two)

¶

¶

¶

¶

For eBooks, never use the Tab Key to start a paragraph or any other task (the right pointing arrow symbol below) it is revealed when you use the Show/Hide feature. They are fine for Print.

→   →

You need a Table of Contents and an Index for non-fiction. For fiction the TOC is optional and the Index is not needed.

For Print, set each chapter title as Heading 1 under the STYLES tab. When you complete your book, go to the REFERENCE tab, set your cursor at the page you wish to have your TOC and click on the first option. A TOC will be generated with the correct page numbers. You can experiment with different styles to find the one that best suits you. The TOC for this book was generated this way.

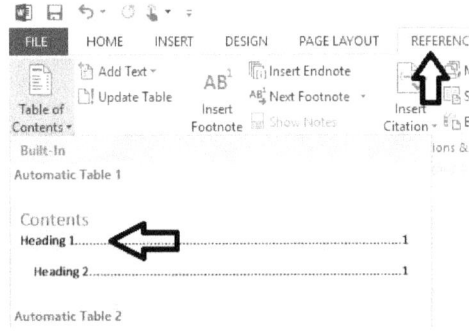

If you need to update your TOC after editing your book, go back to the TOC you created and right mouse click on it. Choose Update Field.

Contents¶

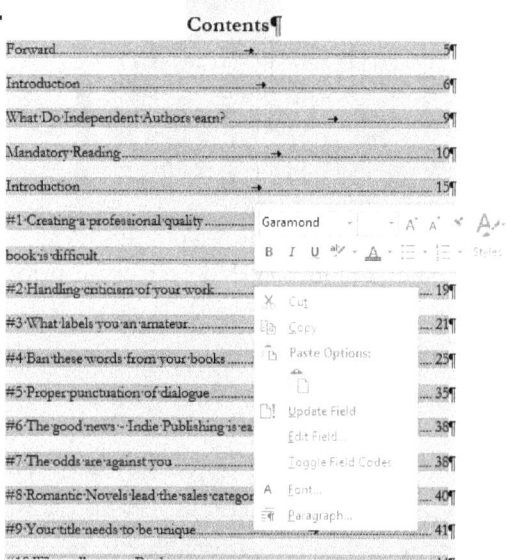

Click on Update Field to reveal a new pop up. When you choose either Update page numbers, the chapter settings will remain the same. If you choose Update entire table, all chapter titles and page number will be updated.

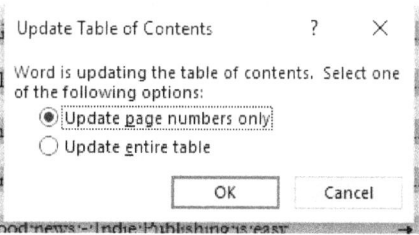

ISBN – The International Standard Book Number is a unique tracking number assigned to a book title by the publisher to help simplify ordering. These are available for free with most publishers. It's imperative that you have one for each title. eBooks and Print have different ISBNs. eBooks and Print have different ISBNs. Below is the ISBN for the print version of this book. They are optional for eBooks.

Page Breaks – I do not recommended breaks for print unless you have a large number of illustrations or photos. Then you will need them to keep the text and image on the correct page. You can not use page breaks for any reason while formatting eBooks.

eBooks require hyperlink Table of Contents rather than the ones found in print with page numbers. The process is daunting for a beginner and too confusing to try to spell out in this book. I suggest that you go to Youtube.com and do a search for "hyperlink table of contents word" You'll find any number of tutorials on how to produce them.

#21 Odds and Ends

Avoid Clichés Like the Plague

Touch base, throw them under the bus, build a nest egg, in the nick of time, it's now or never, only time will tell, at the speed of light, a diamond in the rough, clear as a bell and my favorite cliché: a picture is worth a thousand words.

The first time someone used these, it was probably clever. Now they're worn out and boring. <u>Get it in gear</u> and create your own catch phrases.

Never start your story with a weather report

"It was a dark and stormy night…"

Bad dialect is poison to your story

Dialogue peppered with apostrophes to denote that a character drops their aitches, or the g at the end of an ing word, for example. Once it's established that's how a person speaks, one simply so needs not to do it. (drop one's aitches fail to pronounce the letter *h* at the beginning of words, a common feature of dialect speech.)

Example: Melanie said, "I don't like 'im 'cause 'e's always sayin' 'e's better than me at talkin'"

If this goes on for more than a sentence or two, it will pull me out of a story.

But – but – but John Steinbeck did it in *Of Mice and Men.*

"No reason at all for you. I like it here. Tomorra we're gonna go to work. I seen thrashin' machines on the way down. That means we'll be bucking grain bags, bustin' a gut. Tonight I'm gonna lay right here and look up. I like it." – *Of Mice and Men*.

1.) You're not John Steinbeck.

2.) This isn't 1930.

Old-Fashioned, really bad Southern Dialect from *Uncle Tom's Cabin* by Harriet Beecher Stowe.

"S'pose we must be resigned; but oh Lord! how ken I? If I know'd anything whar you's goin', or how they'd sarve you! Missis says she'll try and 'deem ye, in a year or two; but Lor! nobody never comes up that goes down thar! They kills 'em! I've hearn 'em tell how dey works 'em up on dem ar plantations."

"There'll be the same God there, Chloe, that there is here."

"Well," said Aunt Chloe, "s'pose dere will; but de Lord lets dreful things happen, sometimes. I don't seem to get no comfort dat way."

Remember

1.) You're not Harriet Beecher Stowe

2.) This isn't 1852 when there were few printed books, few who were literate and even fewer who had all day to read and study a page in depth.

3.) You want to give your characters unique voices while still giving your reader an enjoyable and smooth reading experience. Achieving that goal is difficult but doable.

How it's done

"Just what are you gaping at?"

"Your cute little tush," Estelline said in her southern twang.

"Very funny."

"Can't help myself. I was just thinking what a good-looking woman you turned out to be. "

From *Ricochet In Time* by Lori L. Lake

Omit the semi colon

;

The Rule: Use a semicolon if the second part of your sentence can stand by itself but is still related to the first part, but in novel writing, it's bad form.

Instead of: "The stranger jogged towards the park; he found a bench and rested."

Consider: "The stranger jogged towards the park. He found a bench and rested."

As Kurt Vonnegut once said,

"Here is a lesson in creative writing. First rule: Do not use semicolons … All they do is show you've been to college."

The semi-colon is a burp, a hiccup. It's a drunk staggering out of the saloon at 2 a.m., grabbing your lapels on the way and asking you to listen to one more story.

Remember, in essays and scholarly writing, the semi-colon does serve a purpose; I've used them myself. In such writings you're often stringing two thoughts together for a larger point, and the semi-colon allows you to clue the reader in on this move.

But in fiction, you want each sentence to stand on its own, boldly. The semi-colon is an invitation to pause, to think twice, to look around in different directions, to wonder where the heck you're standing.

"Do you want that? Or do you want your story to move?"
Joe Monroe in the Kill Zone.

Set up Spelling and Grammar Check

Under the FILE Tab click on PROOFING

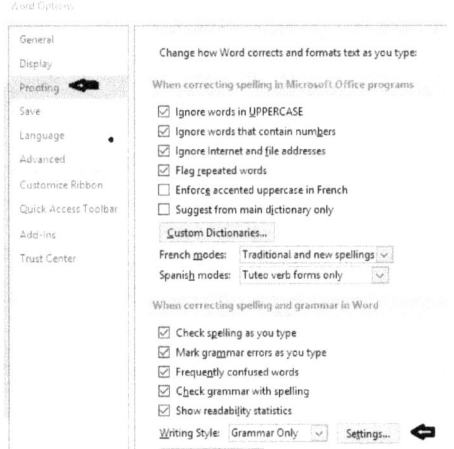

Then click on Settings. Check off most of the options as I have done.

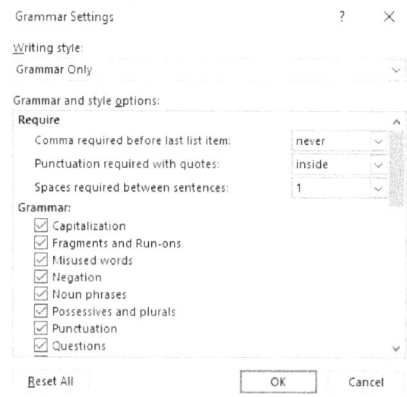

Mistakes will appear with underlines. Right mouse click on them to reveal the error. Once you have made these corrections, you'll be less inclined to make them in the future. The sentence underlined below is a fragment and you should fix them.

Keep in mind that in novel writing, sentence structure is relaxed due to the characters speech patterns. In nonfiction the rules apply.

Correct: This experience has motivated me to outline my background and qualifications, to earn the right to offer you my advice.

Grammar Settings ? ✕

Writing style:

Grammar Only ⌄

Grammar and style options:

Style: ⌃
- ☐ Clichés, Colloquialisms, and Jargon
- ☐ Contractions
- ☐ Fragment - stylistic suggestions
- ☐ Gender-specific words
- ☑ Hyphenated and compound words
- ☑ Misused words - stylistic suggestions
- ☐ Numbers
- ☑ Passive sentences
- ☐ Possessives and plurals - stylistic suggestions
- ☑ Punctuation - stylistic suggestions
- ☑ Relative clauses - stylistic suggestions
- ☑ Sentence length (more than sixty words)
- ☑ Sentence structure ⌄

Reset All · OK · Cancel

Grammar Settings ? ✕

Writing style:

Grammar Only ⌄

Grammar and style options:
- ☑ Passive sentences ⌃
- ☐ Possessives and plurals - stylistic suggestions
- ☑ Punctuation - stylistic suggestions
- ☑ Relative clauses - stylistic suggestions
- ☑ Sentence length (more than sixty words)
- ☑ Sentence structure
- ☑ Sentences beginning with And, But, and Hopefully
- ☑ Successive nouns (more than three)
- ☑ Successive prepositional phrases (more than three)
- ☑ Unclear phrasing
- ☑ Use of first person
- ☑ Verb phrases - stylistic suggestions
- ☑ Wordiness
- ☑ Words in split infinitives (more than one) ⌄

Reset All · OK · Cancel

Conquer Writers' Block with Odd News

https://www.yahoo.com/news/odd/

Thieves Steal Only the Fake Phones at a Verizon...

wafflesatnoon.com/thieves-steal-fake-phones...

Thieves who attempted a "smash and grab" attempt at a Verizon store steal only the fake phones at a Verizon store

I used this news article as a foundation for a short story, The Heist (later story changed to *A Dark and Stormy Night* as a working title)

I didn't know how to expand the story, then found this

Alaska inmate escapes, then comes back to try to free others

FAIRBANKS, Alaska (AP) — A minimum-security prisoner who escaped from a halfway house in Alaska came back three hours later, but it wasn't to turn himself in. -- Associated Press

Now I have Part II to my short story and will expand it to a novel.

Other Odd News

Firefighters rescue naked man from Iowa business's chimney

CARROLL, Iowa (AP) — Carrie Sapp teased her husband, Brad, about being afraid of ghosts when he said he heard someone whisper "get out of here" while he was sorting cans at his Iowa recycling business. Of course it wasn't a ghost. It was a naked man in the chimney. Associated Press

Other Sources

http://www.upi.com/Odd_News/

Welsh sheep go on rampage after eating cannabis plants

About Smashwords.com

FOR AUTHORS, PUBLISHERS AND LITERARY AGENTS, Smashwords offers quick and easy eBook distribution to most of the world's largest eBook retailers. We provide free tools for marketing, distribution, metadata management and sales reporting. At Smashwords, our authors and publishers have complete control over the sampling, pricing and marketing of their written works. Smashwords is ideal for publishing novels, short fiction, poetry, personal memoirs, monographs, non-fiction, research reports, essays, or other written forms that haven't even been invented yet.

KDP Amazon

Independently publish with Kindle Direct Publishing to reach millions of readers.

Get to market fast. Publishing takes less than 5 minutes and your book appears on Kindle stores worldwide within 24-48 hours.

Make more money. Earn up to 70% royalty on sales to customers in the US, Canada, UK, Germany, India, France, Italy, Spain, Japan, Brazil, Mexico, Australia and more. Enroll in KDP Select and earn more money through Kindle Unlimited and the Kindle Owners' Lending Library.

Keep control. Keep control of your rights and set your own list prices. Make changes to your books at any time.

Get started today! Publish your books with KDP Proper format

Createspace.com

Through our services, you can sell books, CDs, and DVDs for a fraction of the cost of traditional manufacturing, while maintaining more control over your materials. We make it simple to distribute your books, music, and video through Internet retail outlets, your own website, and other bookstores, retailers, libraries, and academic institutions. Get started today!

Createspace is a DBA of On-Demand Publishing LLC, part of the Amazon group of companies.

Paid Services: I do not recommend any services that will publish and market your book for a fee. Maintain control and maximize your royalties by using one of the free services above.

#21 ½ My Published Writers

This incomplete chapter contains a partial list of my fellow writers who published their books after taking my classes. I wish to acknowledge their hard work and patience as they plowed through a myriad of technical and often times a tedious process, but persevere they did.

I will update this book each year to reflect changes in the market and process along with more published works.

Please contact me at mike@swedenberg.com if you have questions or feedback on this material.

MY LUPUS JOURNEY is a story about the time Aimee was diagnosed with Lupus and how she weathered many trials and challenges on her journey of twenty years with the disease.

Aimee Ackell

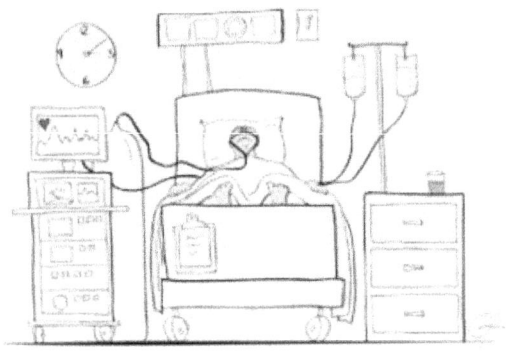

Recovering From Heart Surgery
Going Home

by
Ira D. Levofsky

"What Mr. Levofsky has done with this book based on his own life and experience with cardiac surgery is very special and will be of help to patients and their support network."

Dr. Daniel Goldman MD, FAAC, FHRS

Major League
Baseball: Revised
Standings 2015 Season

PETER WALTON

An innovative, in-depth system where the MLB playoff teams will be determined via democracy.

Peter Walton

Hoping she would have made Erma Bombeck proud, Nancy writes about her everyday life with an openness, wit and humor that keeps readers wanting more.

Nancy H. Lopez

The author draws upon the skills and knowledge she has gained and as well as the real-life experiences of her extended family, friends and co-workers to give men and women of all generations the tools, tips, insights and motivation to succeed.   Helen Fletschinger

MAKE THE MOST OF YOUR 20's! Your decisions will impact your long-term health, finances, relationships, and fulfillment. With the book's inspiring stories and "customize your life" activities, you're on your way to a happier life

Irene Caniano

INDEX

Answer Key

Dialogue punctuation worksheet

Insert quote marks and commas in the proper place

"Take the train to town. It's faster."

"She called you," Randy said, "but you didn't care."

"He called you."

"He called you?" Brenda asked, the loathing clear in her voice and posture.

"He called you," Francis said.

Anna said, "Let's leave now."

"Bill called you," Dorothy said, hoping Brenda didn't hear her."

Walking towards Steven, she said, "He called you."

"Frankie called you," Jose said, but you let it go to voicemail.

"Tony called you." Amy said, hoping to provoke anger. "But you let it go to voicemail."

ABOUT THE AUTHOR

Mike Swedenberg has been self-publishing books for over five years. He provides copywriting, coaching and teaches continuing education classes at Nassau Community College. His educational background in business, sales, creative writing and marketing has given him a broad base from which to approach many topics. His writing skills are confirmed independently on Amazon.com He especially enjoys producing study guides and self-help books.

You may learn more about him at his Pinterest account: https://www.pinterest.com/mikeswedenberg

Sam Chinkes
Las Vegas, NV.

www.ingramcontent.com/pod-product-compliance
Lightning Source LLC
Chambersburg PA
CBHW060403190526
45169CB00002B/723